Kelly

YOUNG WRITERS

WRITE AND SHINE

NORTH WALES

First published in Great Britain in 1995 by
POETRY NOW
1-2 Wainman Road, Woodston,
Peterborough, PE2 7BU

SB ISBN 1 85731 539 1

Foreword

Cock-a-doodle-doo, wakey wakey, write and shine!

Welcome to this selection of poems by young writers from your area. The poems you are about to read express thoughts and feelings on a wide range of themes which are close to the poets' hearts. All the poems in this anthology vary in style, content and subject and we hope that you enjoy reading them as much as we did editing them.

So why don't you start your day with a generous serving of poems drenched in imagination and topped with a sprinkling of emotion.

Sarah Andrew
Editor

CONTENTS

School	Name	No.
Penweddig School		
	Zöe Morris	51
	Bethan Jenkins	52
Dyffryn Ogwen School		
	Frances Hebenstreit	53
St Gerard's School		
	Catriona Duffy	54
	Charlotte Tivy-Jones	54
	Michael Gardener	55
	Bethan Weedon	56
	Sarah Williams	56
	Helen Coates	57
	Sarah Hennessey	58
	Phoebe Hale	58
	Erika Boe	59
	Charlotte Handby	60
	Elizabeth Boddington	60
	Rachel Bacon	61
	Carol Young	61
	Nichola Raihani	62
	Kate Magee	62
	Kate Wilkinson	63
	Katie Jenkins	64
	Laura Owen	64
	Marie-Anne Witcombe	65
	Richard Waterton	66
	Melanie Burroughs	66
	Josephine Connolly	67
	Richard Finch	67
	Gareth Jones	68
	Rhiannon Jones	68
	Emma Verghese	69
	James Williams	69
	John Gardener	70
	Catherine Field	71
	Stephanie Parry	71
	Sharita Oomeer	72
	Fay Josephy	73

John Beddoes School

GOLDILOCKS AND THE THREE BEARS

One night on a sunny day
three bears was walking away
they went for a walk
and they were having a talk
when they went Goldilocks appeared
She has grown a big brown beard
This time she walked in
She went straight to the bread bin
to have some bread
She tried a bit then she was dead
The bears came home
To find her there
She was dead under the chair
they tried to wake her
she wouldn't wake
They left her there
And they had some cake
They phoned for the ambulance 999
then they were waiting wasting time
then the ambulance came
She did not look the same
They took her away
And there was nothing else to say.
They went inside to play Nintendo
They forgot about Goldilocks
They put on the door bolts and locks
They sat down to watch the box
Then they put on the bedtime socks
And they went to bed.

Nia Lewis (12) Gwendraeth Valley Comprehensive School

THE THREE BEARS

There was a family of bears
Who had a house with stairs
One day they thought they'd hunt for food
Oh yes, they were in the wood

As the bears went on their travel
A little girl thought she'd unravel
Her name was Goldilocks
What a disgusting girl
She picks her nose
It could make you hurl

She entered the house
There was nobody there
She walked into the house
Playing with her hair

In come the bears
She's caught in the act
The bears have a check
Thank God everything's intact

The bears are mad they roar so high
Goldilocks grabs a poker
And stabs him in the eye
The poker drops she makes a runner
The cops are there she's a goner

Richard Jones (13) Gwendraeth Valley Comprehensive School

SIXTH FORM STRESS

Work, work,
It's driving me berserk!
Muddled over options,
Should I drop, and swap some?

Stress, stress,
Just relax and do your best.
It's time to pause and think -
Feels like my brain is on the blink!

Scream, shout,
Just let your worries out.
Stick to it, things will soon pick up,
Just don't ever think of giving up.

By a thoroughly confused sixth former!

Sally Pettiford (16) Gwendraeth Valley Comprehensive School

END OF THE WORLD

Perfect world, green with sunlight,
Cloudy blue skies, shiny silver river,
Wind blowing warm through white blossom
Dreamy blue-bell filled forest
Happy, overjoyed, great to be alive.

Church bells tolled in gloomy light,
Nuclear explosion, flying glass
Nothing matters in this unreal atmosphere
A one room shelter from danger
Don't bother, end of the world.

Anwen Terry (14) Gwendraeth Valley Comprehensive School

THE TOLLING OF THE BELLS - ENCHANTED FOREST

A summer stroll of self indulgence,
Quiet as a millpond, eight bells toll,
Idle dawnlight lingers on the horizon,
The benevolent forest awakens.

Overlaying the rustic quietude,
An eternal hush . . . still dead.
Asylum has been granted,
Inviting all who dare to enter.

Deeper goes the primrose path,
Drawing closer to the heart,
Petrified trees shrink with fear,
Bloodied poppies shed a tear . . .
. . . Evil dwells . . . somewhere near.

Stirring the bedrock foundations,
Something dormant, famished and old.
Silently murmurs, dark and cold,
Shattering the solitude . . . the evil awakes . . .

. . . Suffocating forest, stream and knoll . . .
. . . Oppressive, claustrophobic . . .
Death bells toll . . .

Sîan Morgan (16) Gwendraeth Valley Comprehensive School

MY IDEA OF HEAVEN

Sea sprayed harbour
Beach and rocks
Sprinkled with glistening droplets,
Sparkling in the sun.
Warm breeze, clear sky,
Waves of heat streaming down,
Waves of sea lapping against sand,
Crashing against rocks.
Deep, clear blue waters,
Dramatic against brilliant white foam.

Harbour wall stretching towards horizon,
Sitting with sea all around me,
Watching . . . Listening . . .
Boats coming and going
Gliding through mysterious, calming waves.
The breath of the wind spraying me
With soft, cool mist of the ocean.
Tresses of hair tickling my face,
Seagulls above screeching to one another,
Skimming over the water.

As the day grows older,
It's now eight o'clock,
I see the sun turn the sea
To a golden, shimmering silk cloth,
Rippling under the gently darkening sky.
As the tide turns towards another coast,
I feel disheartened now to know
That we both must leave this heaven.

Angela Williams (17) Gwendraeth Valley Comprehensive School

BEAUTY AND THE DESTROYED

A perfect day, birds of a feather,
Trees of all weather, flowers bunched together,
Grass glittering through the morning.
Bees and butterflies looking for nectar.
Oh what a world so full and tender.

What has become of this world?
Machines and computers
Humans tearing the land,
Trees cut down for paper,
Elephants killed, species extinct,
Computers running our brains.
War after war,
Shooting after shooting,
Humans getting killed,
A world that was full of beauty
Now full of anger.

Paul Davies (14) Gwendraeth Valley Comprehensive School

IMAGES

The pretty lights on the dark tree,
Seem to magnify every thing - times two or three
Against the wall, the shadows grow
Familiar Christmas figures we all know

Angels like monsters, baubles like cannon balls
Chasing the poor teddy bears up the scarred walls
The Christmas presents, to the tree they bind,
And seem to enthral a little child's mind.

The chocolate barrels chase poor old Santa,
The elves run, the reindeer canter,
They don't scare me, they're only images,
Yes that's right, they're only images

Jayne Anslow (14) Gwendraeth Valley Comprehensive School

THE END OF THE WORLD

A perfect day, promise of summer.
Cloudless blue sky, swallows nesting
River estuary shining silver.
Gloucester green in the sunlight, blackbirds singing
Wind blowing warm through hair.
Roadside lacy with cow parsley,
May covered hedges with sweet white blossoms.
Cattle grazing in fields, as the kestrel hovers above.
Woods dreamy with bluebells.
Cuckoo calling through silence.
Washing billowing in gardens,
Church bells tolling in the distance
Sunlight among the apple leaves,
Sheep bleating on the common, below the heavenly blue sky.

Nerys Jones (14) Gwendraeth Valley Comprehensive School

HEAVEN

Hot derelict Caribbean bay
Black thoroughbred
Galloping through clear blue sea
Thundering hooves
Against splashes of sea water
Warm breeze
Flowing loose hair
Speed and adrenaline
Rushing through my body
A dark figure emerges
Distantly watching
From the shade of palm trees

Natalie Hyde (17) Gwendraeth Valley Comprehensive School

THE NUCLEAR WAR

Perfect day,
Promise of summer,
Cloudless blue skies above,
River shining silvery in the distance.
Smell of honeysuckle
Hedges covered with sweet white blossom
Bluebirds singing in a chorus
Bluebells covering evergreen woods
Sheep bleating happily,
Cows resting silently.
Monday's washing billowing in the gardens
Warm wind,
Whispering through your ears.
Bright bloomy colours
Fiery yellow sun.
Buttercups on the grass
A carpet of shimmering gold.
Was it a rumble of thunder
Maybe nuclear explosions
Waves of sound sweeping everywhere.
Skies turn from blue to black.
Families in houses,
Huddled in one room.
Scared to breath or move.
Like a hurricane
Tearing trees,
Whirling leaves.
Sky, wind and fire.
Screams of fright.
Cries of horror
Hearts thumping like the bonging of drums
The nuclear war was here.

Houses destroyed
Tragic deaths
Suddenly stillness
The war was over
But the death had just began.

Kelly Stephens (14) Gwendraeth Valley Comprehensive School

THE END OF THE WORLD

A perfect day, a promise of summer,
Cloudless blue skies, swallows nesting.
First bombs fallen, Hamburg, Leningrad,
Full scale nuclear attack, imminent.
Go home immediately, the rest to remain,
A town gone mad with panic.
The traffic had stopped, cars, lorries,
Parked along the narrow streets.
Men and women crazy with fear,
Looting the shops for supplies.
Police sirens sounded, tearing doors from hinges,
Boarding up windows.
Shoes pounded along the pavements,
Blackbird singing, wind blowing warm.
Birmingham has been hit,
The electric light gloomy, unreal.
A rumble in the distance,
Roof tiles smashed, windows blown inward.
A brief glimpse of devastation,
A hurricane, tearing trees and whirling leaves.
Things sank back into stillness,
It is over, it's just the beginning.

Richard Morgan (14) Gwendraeth Valley Comprehensive School

THE END OF THE WORLD

There was no light
Just total darkness
Children are bored
Noise of bombs and guns
In the total silence
Of the household

All worlds beautiful
Dead beneath the dust
Trees cut down for paper
Humans tearing up land
For all kinds of adventures

War after war
Bomb shells everywhere
Shooting all the time
Earth's beauties
Never to be seen again

Alex Evans (14) Gwendraeth Valley Comprehensive School

MR WILLIAMS

Mr Williams is a marching tune,
Driving us to work.
He is a cold autumn night,
Killing trees, leaves, bushes, us.
In the middle of a war
Pushing everybody into death.

He is a cold windy day,
Pushing everyone around.
He is a pair of roller skates,
Taking us everywhere
A tank, killing everything in sight,
Fully armed to kill.

Mark Coleman (13) Gwendraeth Valley Comprehensive School

THE END OF THE WORLD

Perfect day, promise of summer
Cloudy blue skies,
Swallows nesting below the eaves
A blackbird singing
Church bells tolled
Two renovated cottages made into one
Buckets filled with water.
Sheep grazing in the field.

Brief glimpse of devastation
The sky had gone black
Bombs fell over Cardiff and Bristol
Barricade shuddered
Broken windows
Then it faded away into silence
Windows were blown inwards
Roof tiles smashed
Bookcase started to topple
Hurricane of tearing trees.
The next wave of sword
The war had ended.

Iwan Lewis (14) Gwendraeth Valley Comprehensive School

PRISON LIFE

That terrible fear
The grey bare rooms
The feeling of escaping
The urge to get away.
But what about the others,
Getting away getting away.
The beat of the guards' footsteps
The darkness of the room
Escape, escape!

Carla Hitchin (12) Gwendraeth Valley Comprehensive School

DAVID IS FREE

Lying still in the darkness,
Listening to men's low muttering,
Aware of their voices.
A silent noise in the distance,
The guard blows his whistle
Out of his bed he ran,
Down the halls and past the cells
A guard was standing there.
He let David pass
What a relief!
David was free!

At long last David was free,
Free to lead his own life,
He wandered out of his prison grounds
Ran with joy and laughter,
Looking around him
There were no webs or rats.
He was out in the wild
Suddenly he tripped,
It was only a sheep
But he thought again
David was free!

Lee Phillips (13) Gwendraeth Valley Comprehensive School

A CONVERSATION

'Where have you been?'
'Down in the shed.'
'What did you say?'
'In the shed, I said.'

'Will you help me?'
'By doing what?'
'Go to the sink
And clean the pot.'

'What is for dinner?'
'Sausages and peas.'
'What is for pudding?'
'Biscuits and cheese.'

'How was your day?'
'It was all right.'
'Are you feeling ill?
You've gone very white.'

'I'd better go back
Out to the garden.
So I'll leave the table
And beg your pardon.'

Anita Ghosh (11) Gwendraeth Valley Comprehensive School

THE FOURTH MEMBER OF THE FAMILY

He stands as tall as he can
Shifting his small body
Into a neat, prim position.
Smiling, blinking eyes
Green and large
Wink back at me
As I talk to him.

Slumbering on the bed,
Limbs outstretched
In a relaxed position.
Totally at ease, except for
The occasional nervous twitch
Of hair or tail
As he dreams on.

Standing on cold blue tiles
His bare feet stomp
Up and down
As he demands food
Bushy tail twice as wide as normal
Quivers impatiently
As I open the tin.

In the dimmed lounge
Eyes glint in the firelight:
I move the string along
As he pounces with gripping paws.
In sinks the claw
Causing me pain, drawing blood
Yet he doesn't even realise.

Caroline Hier (18) Gwendraeth Valley Comprehensive School

DISREGARDED

Frowned over by mountains,
The grieving gulls circle
above the rubbish strewn beach,
the ears of the human
deaf to the mournful cries.

The human child lies alone,
protected by cardboard
from the lament of the wind,
the ears of the human
deaf to the mournful cries.

Tears thrown by weeping sea,
hit the meagre shelter
and easily penetrate,
the ears of the human
deaf to the mournful cries.

Though too young to understand,
not too young to suffer,
the human baby struggled,
the ears of the world were
deaf to the mournful cries.

Emma Thomas (17) Gwendraeth Valley Comprehensive School

PRISON LIFE

David lay quite still in the darkness
Men's low muttering
Grey bare room
Vague meaningless noise
Corner of the grey room
Swings the beam

Beauty and freedom.

Several hours passed

So cold
No-one to disturb his sleep that night
All was quiet
Grey and brown and a blue sky
One red flower on the camp wall
The sea, a sea bluer than any sky
All green and golden
Red flowers spread across the land
Colours gleamed dazzlingly
Trees changing hints of green
Shone the warming sun
Spiteful and scorching.

Katie Smithson (12) Gwendraeth Valley Comprehensive School

I AM DAVID

Grey bare rooms
Black blank ceilings
Staring, staring
in a trance
Cold and shivery a musty
smell.
No-one to talk to
Going crazy inside
knowing knowing
you'll never get out.

Green, blue, yellow, red.
Big curving rainbows
in a blue blue sky
Happy, happy to be free
No more ceilings
No more grey
Birds are singing
in the trees
flying, flying
up so high

Gemma Davies (12) Gwendraeth Valley Comprehensive School

I AM DAVID

Lying, still in darkness
In a grey, bare room
Trapped inside,
Inside the prison
Terror and hatred,
Locked away in your mind,
Locked up in an inky-blackness,
With nothing
And no-one.

Bright colours,
Flowers and trees,
A shining blue sky
Green grass and a blazing sun,
Beautiful scenery,
And freedom,
Free at last.

Laura Bowen (12) Gwendraeth Valley Comprehensive School

IS THAT ME?

Is that me standing there
All dressed up in white
Tinsel on my shoes and hair
And thick white woolly tights.

Is that Sam dressed as an elf
With bobbles on his toes
Next to me with a cheeky grin
And a little button nose

Is that me standing there?

Alexandra Fuge (13) Gwendraeth Valley Comprehensive School

DIFFERENT WORLDS

David lay still
On his bed
In the darkness
Of the camp.
The camp had been
His life ever since
He began;
All he sees is
Darkness and his
Memories.

Freedom is magical;
Walking freely through
The fields running
Jumping, freedom
Is so wonderful
For the first time
In my life, I heard
The birds singing
In the trees freely.
Freedom is wonderful.

Gareth Richards (12) Gwendraeth Valley Comprehensive School

A FAIR

Loud music, bright lights,
People screaming with delight,
Hot-dogs and candyfloss,
Dodgem cars and carousels,
Homeward bound with happy faces,
Sleepy eyes and empty pockets.

Dylan Eynon (11) Gwendraeth Valley Comprehensive School

MEMORY

My memory of America
Is very plain
I wish I could go there
Once again
So much to do, different places
Lots of people, colours, races

The water was still and cool
As I lay there beside the
Pool
The sun beamed down on
My face
So I put sunblock on, just in case

The night life was amazing
Big building bright lights all glazing
Big scary rides
Coasters shoots and slides
Laughter giggles and screams
Imagine it in your wildest dreams

Kirsty Richards (13) Gwendraeth Valley Comprehensive School

THE END OF THE WORLD

promise of summer
cloudless, perfect blue skies
sweet smelling blossoms
fields of dreamy bluebells

nuclear winters
blackened out sun
diseased smell of death
land of charcoaled bodies

rivers shining silver
emerald green trees
leaves glimmering in the sun

thick soup like waters
charcoaled black trees
leaves burnt out and colourless

Dee Lewis (14) Gwendraeth Valley Comprehensive School

IS THAT ME

Is that me?
with the cheeky grin
wearing a red velvet dress
with little frills.

Is that me?
wearing red shiny shoes
and thick woolly tights
my hair is almost
out of sight.

Ruth James (13) Gwendraeth Valley Comprehensive School

I AM DAVID

Cold night people muttering
Moon shining into the dark room
Staring at walls
Muttering closer, steps louder fear increases
Walking back step after step
Until you get to the wall
Crouched down steps
Faster and louder
There, a big tall man
Big, shiny boots
Staring at you
Walk on rattling the cages.

Gavin Griffiths (12) Gwendraeth Valley Comprehensive School

IS THAT ME?

Is that me sitting on my mother's
    lap,
With no hair I wish I wore a
    cap.
Is that me with feet the size of
    a grown up's thumb,
Why am I looking like that
    at my mum
Is that me with that little
    head,
I think I'm tired and want
    to got to bed.
Is that me with that tiny
    nose,
Whoever took this photo could
    have told me to pose.

Rhian Hughes (13) Gwendraeth Valley Comprehensive School

I AM DAVID

Prison,
Dark, cold,
Misty all night,
Lonely and noisy,
Not a soul in sight,
Nothing to say,
Nothing to read,
Even though I won't be there.

Beauty, freedom,
What a lovely sight,
Far below lay the sea,
A sea bluer than any sky,
Red flowers too far to reach,
Coast curving along the shore,
Mountains far away as can be,
Nicer than any other place can be.

Llinos Richards (12) Gwendraeth Valley Comprehensive School

MEMORIES

Is that me with the curly hair,
Wearing a sleepsuit that is blue and pink?
Is that me with my big brown bear,
And my ladybird buggy, let me think?

Look at my face giving someone a
frown
And my chin nearly dragging the floor,
Look at the carpet, it's green white and brown
That's definitely not me anymore!

Rachel Underwood (13) Gwendraeth Valley Comprehensive School

QUENDOS

Spooky, silvery landscape,
Souls of the dead lurking in the
Unilluminated planet,
Where the sun's very aquatic,
Shortened days, bleak nights,
No escape from a sensation of cold.

Green turf, flowing rivers,
Where lives a kind of fish,
Now pacifism, harmony, beauty,
Hopefully now it'll be forever.

Cold blue eyes returns,
Mountains quiver, ice forms,
Rivers freeze.

Rhian Hughes (13) Gwendraeth Valley Comprehensive School

THE FOXHUNT

Poor little critter,
Running for his life.
Brown huge monster,
And his owner's got a knife.
He's orange with a bushy tail,
And hasn't got a chance,
Because the monster's little friends,
Are catching up too fast.

The critters run behind a hedge,
And only just escaped.
The evil jaws of a creature,
That loves to bark and play.

Tracy Henry (11) Gwendraeth Valley Comprehensive School

MR NOBODY

Mr Nobody is sometimes there,
And sometimes not,
He can even fit into the tea pot
His shadows run across the wall
Sometimes thin
And sometimes small,
He hides the brush,
And takes the keys,
In places where no human sees,
It's him that eats
the best choc bar
And leaves the lid off the honey jar
He hides my socks
And moves my shoes till sometimes
We can't see who's is who's
He stays up till late at night
but he's never around
when it's light
Who is this person they all blame
No don't tell me
Mr Nobody again.

Natalie Boyd (12) Gwendraeth Valley Comprehensive School

A FAIR

I came down to earth in a space-ship
From way up in Mars.

I landed in a very strange place,
With machines and games.

There was edible pink cotton wool,
And nuts to knock down

There were long machines driving along
Long winding ladders.

A group of people with strange objects
Were making an odd noise.

I was sitting on a moving wheel,
On a hanging creature.

Anita Ghosh (11) Gwendraeth Valley Comprehensive School

PLANET

Spooky, silvery, landscape,
Souls of the dead lurking in
Unilluminated planet outside
From the cold there is no escape
A sense of death everywhere
The planet is dark and bleak
The sun is pale and watery.

The sun has come, the planet changes
Green grass and flowers appear.
There are lakes, rivers, even fish
There is peace and tranquillity.

Cold blue eyes returns
Mountains quiver, ice forms, rivers
freeze.

Alexandra Fuge (13) Gwendraeth Valley Comprehensive School

THE MAN

I was walking through the woods one day
And I saw a man in the trees
The man was big and very tall
And knobbly at the knees.

Hello, I said to the very tall man
But he did not reply
Why, don't you answer me, mister man
Or are you very shy?

I bent down and touched his arm
But to my great surprise
He flew away with grace and charm
So much so he deceived my eyes.

Then suddenly I realised
It had all been a dream
For where else would I have had these thoughts
Except for in my dreams.

Joanne Brindley (13) Netherwood School

CHRISTMAS DAY

C akes and nice mince pies
H ats from our crackers, we sit
R ound the table, wreaths of
I vy and holly all around
S isters, cousins and brothers
*T*alking about their
M any presents. Uncles and
A unts have come to
S tay. They help gran cook the
D elicious foods and
A fterwards we play games.
Y ear after year it's the same.

Kathryn Hurlock (13) Netherwood School

ELIMINATION OF LIFE

I've been cooped in this small, square,
miserable place, for two days.
Two nights of restless sleep
Worrying, waiting, wondering . . .

My friends? They're dead and gone,
a death that was not called for.
I know I'm to join them soon
and for all the wrong reasons.
I don't want my life to end this way.
I've never done anything to you
You're bigger, stronger . . .

For the sake of looking beautiful;
In the hope of looking good.
Creatures are taken away from this land
If I could I'd put an end to it.
Surely there could be another way.
Injecting, spraying.
Hurting is what they're doing.
Ruining our bodies making them unfit to live
Some of them care, but that's only some.
Those in the white don't.

As the sun rises a new day begins;
in a few hours the lights will flicker on and
the rain begin.
I, as one of the laboratory animals.
lie in my cold, unloving cage.
Worrying, waiting, wondering . . .

Charlotte O'Connor (12) Netherwood School

THE ACCIDENT

Aarrgh . . . Splash, then total immersion.
The iciness and force of the water, my heart was
pounding, as I was torn and crushed against
the rocks. Suddenly I was launched onto
the impenetrable ground, I lay still barely able
to move. I had the feelings of death creeping in
on me. Intense pain, hypothermia, as I lay
by the river, penetrating rain in the
intimidating night. No energy to breathe.

My wounded body, so cold and helpless, no
life to give. Why me . . . I thought, as I lay in
the dark. Out of the night, there came a
blinding light. It drove past, stopped. I heard
footsteps, muttering. They came to me, I fell
asleep, and I was carried away in the midst
of night. When I awoke I was in intensive
care, surgeons, the sound of operating tools.

Mum . . I said, I was alone in a desolate room
with the busy sound beyond the door.
Occasionally listening to the rhythm of my
heart beat on the monitor. After three weeks
I was discharged. I now lead a normal
happy life. But I still have memories of
that traumatic time.

Victoria James (12) Netherwood School

SUMMER

After spring comes summer,
Bringing her long days,
To play in, and her short nights,
To sleep in.
The summer days are beautiful,
Filled with flowers,
The song of birds, and
Chattering of animals.
This is the season for
Long seaside holidays,
Spent lying on the beach
Sunning yourself while
Your kids play on the beach
And in the sea.
Summer seems to pass so
Quickly, before you know it it's
Autumn.
And summer is gone.

Sonia Curry (13) Netherwood School

LONELINESS

I'm just an old man,
Sitting all alone,
Not able to get up,
Just staring at the walls of stone.

Thinking of the old times,
Thinking of the past,
Thinking up answers,
To questions never asked.

I'm just an old man,
Sitting all alone,
All my sons and daughters
Having left home.

Wondering what will happen to me,
Wondering when I'll die,
Only summoning up the strength
To let out a little sigh.

Then one day comes
Different from the others,
I hear a voice say
Something to his brothers.

They're coming this way,
Right up to my chair,
Chattering to me,
Answering my prayer

They put me by the fire
In their comfortable home
Never again will I be,
A man all alone.

Rebecca Evans (12) Netherwood School

THE DREAM

I fell into a hazy dream where everything
Seemed so real. I was falling fast down a
Long steep slope when something grabbed me at
The throat.
The grip was tight and very strong then
I knew there was something wrong.
When I looked up, to my surprise, there was
A great big eagle with smiling eyes.
He jerked me up while in the air and
Before I knew it he had me by the hair
We were flying fast and very high.
I really thought we were going to die.
Round the bushes through the trees, the
Eagle flew with grace and ease.
He threw me up in the air so I
Tossed and turned without a care,
I was falling down on my own oh how
I wished I was not alone.
I woke up with a big fast jerk.
In my house where that big old eagle
No longer lurked.

Fenella Richards (12) Netherwood School

IN PRISON AGAIN

Oh it looks like I'm in prison again
what's dad going to say to Christine?
What were you doing at that time?
I told you to be in at ten!

No-one ever asks me what I want
life is just not fair
I do this because *none* of them ever listen to me

I'm gonna escape
and find a new home
whether they like it or not
A new home for me and just me
no parents and *no* prison!

Rhys Elliott (12) Netherwood School

THE RAILWAY TRAMP

The station was shut,
the night was cold,
the moonbeams shone
on the tracks like gold.
The silence was broken
as an old man stirred,
his name was unknown,
as he never said a word.
He was alone at the station,
he was always there,
with piercing blue eyes
and old greying hair.
The children made fun of him,
they laughed and they taunted,
but all from a distance,
they thought it was haunted.
They thought he was stupid,
that he wouldn't mind,
their words were harsh
and never kind.
But what they never saw when they left the place,
was that a single tear rolled down his face.

Sophie Dyas (16) Netherwood School

THE SNAIL

With twisting shell and slimy
tail,
She is the quiet, gentle snail,
She slips along, round rocks,
through grass
There is nothing that she
cannot pass,
Round a bottle, over a match,
Her destination, the lettuce
patch,
A few hours later,
Journey's end is in sight,
She might just make it
before the night,
On she goes,
Round another stone,
Carrying the burden of her
travelling home.

Sophie Hall (13) Netherwood School

RIP

'May his soul rest in peace.'
The vicar said,
As they lowered my brother
Into his grave.

We threw in some earth,
And left him to rest.
He was such a sensible boy.
Apart from that one time.

He liked to be with his *mates*.
They did everything together.
Oh why did he try the drugs
He was only 10.

They said it would help him,
They were wrong!
They said that a little wouldn't hurt him,
They were wrong!

So there he lies
Alone in his grave,
Where are his *mates* now?
Yes, where are his *mates!*

James Hatton (15) Netherwood School

CHRISTMAS

This is a happy time of
year. This is when drunk
people go on to the streets
and cheer. Christmas is
about Jesus Christ the Lord
and people say they don't
got to church because they
get bored.
It is also based on a
big red fat man all
happy and red faced.
And we eat turkey, chicken
and ham all to celebrate
this man and his name
is Father Christmas

Geraint D Smith (12) Netherwood School

THE SEA

The sea is weird,
lurking with danger,

its murky grey waters,
look foreign and frightened.

Its rogue is unknown;
but seen many times.

For the sea tells lies,
and is not to be trusted.

When you're riding with the sea,
be prepared for surprises,

For the sea is weird,
and lurking with danger.

Richard Perry (13) Netherwood School

MY WORLD

My world is dark and light,
Warm and cold,
But has no detail.

I feel the rain
But I do not see the clouds,
Or the sky that they're in.

I feel the wind
And hear the leaves move
But I can't see the trees.

I've never seen the trees.
I've never seen the sky.
Ever since I was born
My world has been different.
My images may be strange
To anyone who doesn't know.

I build pictures
With my hands,
By touch.

I imagine faces
By the tune of the
Voice I hear.

Everyone says I'm different.
Yes, I am.
I cannot see the people talking.
The reason - I am blind.

Maudie Miller (15) Netherwood School

A STALEMATE

Bombs, mortars, guns,
Snipers shoot down a flicker,
Blood, here and there,
When will it all end?

People in the streets,
Scavenging to survive,
Their lives at risk, from a thread,
But still their families cry.

Children see them fall,
Children see it all,
Children are scared, of being shot,
From the buildings, next door.

People lying dead,
Blood's flowing from their corpses,
But no-one cares enough to help,
Just watch as they writhe in pain.

Soldiers, here and up a tree,
Shoot just for fun,
But do they think about the person's families?
Do they think what they have done.

A game of chess,
Is now in session,
But no-one can win,
It is a lifelong stalemate of stupidity.

Bombs, mortars, guns,
Snipers shoot down a flicker,
Blood here and there,
When will it end? And where?

Liam Hovey (13) Netherwood School

DEATH

She used to read to me
when I was lonely.
Bedtime stories about when
she was a little girl

She was always there for me
every time I was unhappy I'd
run to her but I can't do
that anymore

I never got a chance to say
'I love you'
'Mum, I love you, are you there?'

Dad there's always dad I hear her
saying but he doesn't care
he doesn't understand
Mum!
Why did you have to die
why couldn't you stay here
and look after me?
Why couldn't someone else's
mother die why you?

I miss you mum oh
how I miss you!
Why don't you say something to
me mum! *Please!*

Hannah Waters (13) Netherwood School

SEASONS - 4 HAIKU

The summer

The sun blazing down
A lonely man was walking
through a sunlit park

The autumn

The leaves dropping down
The golden colour is crisp
The trees bare lonely

The winter

The snow is falling
Softly it lands on the ground
Layers of snow, *cold!*

The spring

The spring means green
green trees standing tall sky high
and the birds singing

Roger James (14) Netherwood School

MOVING HOUSE

Pack this, throw it away, it's really strange
We're leaving, leaving it all behind
Getting back to nature so they say.

Having to make new friends, it's not easy
Wales, of all places why so far away!
Don't worry they say things will be alright

No-one asked if I wanted to move
They just said it one night
Will things ever work out

Why? They said at school why?
What can I say they won't, don't understand.
It's hurting everyone hurting me

It's time I've got to be moving on
I'll never be the same again
It's time to say goodbye.

Jacqueline Brown (13) Netherwood School

THE HUNCHBACK

There was a hunchback,
Whose name was Jack,
He was kinda mean
and kinda green.

Now he roamed the castle,
For somebody to haunt,
But he thought it was a bit of a
hassle.

So he went to bed,
and took off his head,
for he thought this was more comfortable
then put it on the table,
till next morning,
when he went a haunting.

Jonathan Powell (12) Netherwood School

GAMBLERS ANONYMOUS

One, two, show me, what I've got,
take me to the slot machines,
you slot to hit the jackpot.
rev it up, rev it up,
come on my Buttercup.
Turn just one more pear, oh no it's got stuck!

Now on the wheel of fortune, a ten comes loud
and clear.
I'm too drunk to say 'All on 10 black'
I'm tanked on drugs and beer!

Gambling here, gambling there,
It's got me in a vice grip,
Snagged me in its snare,
Just one more try, give it all I got,
give me one more thousand, so I can have a shot!
The dice is rollin', my six is in the
bag!
'Oh no' she's got the 10 of hearts, another
major snag,
So now I've gone bankrupt, I'm broke, kapeesh,
caput!
All my money's down the drain,
I'm bankrupt, kapeesh . . .
. . . *caput!* . . .

Scott Francis (13) Netherwood School

TRAVELLING

Along the bendy, windy roads,
Up the hills and through pot-holes,
Through some forests, through the towns,
Up down, up down, up down.

Over the bridge, see the river below,
We're back on the mainland, on we go!

Stop for a snack at the services,
For a couple of chips and a slap up drink!

Coming out feeling full and content,
It's ten to eight and it's getting late,
So get in the car and step on the gas,
And after an hour you arrive, at last!

Matthew Thatcher (11) Netherwood School

WEATHER

Weather is cold
Weather is warm
Weather is all sorts

In the winter the animals
hibernate. In the summer
they wake up again.

In the spring the trees
start to blossom. In
the autumn trees go bare
but the leaves gain nice
colour.

Weather is cold
Weather is warm
Weather is all sorts.

Kimberly King (11) Netherwood School

MY DOG

He's golden and fluffy
my little dog Taffy
He likes to chase cats
and blown away hats.
But he doesn't like the rain
which makes him such a pain
As he won't go out the door
oh he is a little bore
He does lots of tricks like
sit and fetch sticks
At 6 o'clock he'll wait
for his dinner to be on the plate

He's golden and fluffy my
little dog Taffy.

I love him!

Gemma Elliott (13) Netherwood School

MY SCHOOL DAYS

You wake up five days a week;
Wondering if you have to go to school this morning,
The answer basically is *yes!* Go and get dressed;
There's nothing wrong with you! *Now go.*

So we go to school!
Now we get in school!
Quickly get our books ready,
And do unfinished homework.

After that you're so tired that you,
Only just make it through the first lessons.
Break helps get your energy back,
Then we have something like double chemistry.

After that you're just so tired,
You just rush down to lunch,
Sit down quickly it's a boiling hot day,
And you've got school dinners.

I would explain the day,
More if I could,
But really!
It's just too! Hard to describe!

Natalie Hogan (12) Netherwood School

PEOPLE

People come in all different shapes and sizes
Some are big
Some are small
Some are fat
Some are thin
Some are kind
Some are mean
Some are scruffy
Some are clean
Some have rich houses
Some live in boxes
Some have flash cars
Some take the bus
Some wear diamond rings
Some don't wear anything
But some people like to live their way and
even though it can be weird and even though
it can be strange
There's just no telling what people are
like.

Anna Barrett (11) Netherwood School

I HATE SCHOOL

There are lots of things I hate
Like Brussels sprouts and boring days out
But there's nothing I hate more than school

Instead of being woken up gently
I get a quilt pulled off my bed, then my mother shouts
'Have you cleaned your teeth dear?
Have you washed behind your ears?' Then I get,
'Come and have your breakfast love,
Hurry up or you'll be late!'

Then I jump into the car 'We'll never make it, it's just too far'
And then I realised I had forgotten my brief case,
Finally we arrived (an hour too late)
I get a quick peck on the cheek, then I was bundled out of
the car.

I dive into the classroom without a single knock
I run inside, tripped and hit my head on the desk
But Mrs Jones was not too impressed
So she sent me away straight to the head.

At last, my favourite lesson, *break!*
I reach into my pocket for my conkers
I was winning until a boy named Bill got in my way,
I hit his head
And I woke up in the matron's bed
With a broken arm and a broken leg
And a very swollen head.
I hate school don't you

David Pye (11) Netherwood School

CHRISTMAS

The winter is here,
The snow is on the ground.
It's almost time for Santa
To begin his Christmas round.

Christmas is almost here, up with
the Christmas tree.
I can't wait to see, all the Christmas
presents for me.

It's Christmas eve, there's not a
leaf on the tree.
I still can't wait to see all the
presents for me.

Christmas is over
The decorations are off the tree.
I've opened all the presents that
were addressed to me.

Jonathan Bury (11) Netherwood School

AUTUMN

Golden leaves are falling,
The rain is falling too,
I hate the rain falling on my head,
But I don't mind the leaves falling too,

Churches full,
Of harvest things,
People rejoicing,
At harvest home

Golden leaves are falling,
The rain is too
I don't mind the leaves falling,
But I hate rain falling on my head,

Soon it will be snow falling,
And winter will follow,
With Christmas not far away,

But for now,
I'm just happy with autumn,
The leaves falling,
And the rain is too,
I'm happy with autumn,
Are you?

Alistair Morris (14) Netherwood School

MOUNTAINS

When spring comes soon to the mountains,
with its streams so cool and clear.
And crystal springs rise in fountains,
I'm close to my heaven here.

In summer I climb to the summit warm,
with the song of birds all around.
And thunder crashes in the summer storm,
summer has such a pleasant sound.

Hills in autumn covered with trees,
their leaves burst into colours so bright.
Autumn to me will always please,
the leaves glowing in the evening light.

Their peaks in winter glow white with snow,
beauty must be at its perfection now.
Hidden by snow icy streams do flow,
with thick coated ice on every tree's bough.

Naomi Mudie (11) Penglais School

QUICK POEM

Five minutes to write a poem!
Wasted the rest trying to think of something to write.
Come on, think of something!
I've only got about one minute left.
I've got something!
I've finally thought of something!
Drrriiinnnggg!
Oh no! The bell!
'Right class, pack away your books'

Ruth Hogg (11) Penglais School

THE HEDGEHOG

At sunset when the night dew falls,
over the ivy by the walls,
with his spears of gold,
and his black shield,
is the hedgehog behold!

As the night draws closer to dawn,
the hedgehog treads across the lawn,
looking for something nice and tender,
like a worm that's long and slender.

As the hedgehog walks sleepily to his den,
just before the wake of men,
through the bushes under the trees,
past the pond and to his den with
Glee!

Rebecca Price (11) Penglais School

I AM A LIGHTHOUSE

I am a lighthouse,
Standing big and strong,
Signalling to all the ships,
All night long.

Sometimes the sea is quiet,
Lapping against the sand,
While sometimes it is noisy,
As loud as a big brass band.

James Davey (11) Penglais School

MARY MARY

Mary Mary quite contrary how does our garden grow?
I live with my rat, in a high rise flat,
So how in the world would I know?

Tony Peter Jones (11) Penglais School

A DRINK CALLED LONELINESS

I see you sat there all alone,
Are you real? Are you stone?

Your eyes stare cold around the room,
Your heart cries out from within its tomb,

Silent lips, do you talk?
Idle legs, do you walk?

I'm distanced from you by years,
But soon enough, I'll share your tears,

The music calls, I go to dance,
You have ears, but not the chance,

Partners many, with faces fair,
But when I leave you're still there,

Life isn't eternal, youth doesn't last,
We all have a present, we all have a past,

Taken over by selflessness,
We all share a drink called loneliness.

Zöe Morris (14) Penweddig School

THE END

In
the tapestry of life
You
were a golden thread which tarnished as it wound its way through
In
the ocean of my life
You
were a welcoming coral reef in which lurked vicious
sharp-toothed sharks
In
the forest of my life
You
were a small song-bird whose songs turned to the screams of
an eagle as you alighted on my hands.
And suddenly you
Ended it.
Not so much announced as hinted,
And so I
Unpicked your golden thread from my tapestry and patched it up,
but still it felt strangely unfinished
I
swam free of your reef and its sharks,
but still I felt unhappy
I
shot the eagle as it sat on my arm,
but still I felt a loss.
and you cried
'Bye!' and let slip the dogs of despair and self-doubt.
You stood watching as they mutilated and dismembered
my self-confidence
and you turned to the mutilated and bloodied remains of my ego
and whispered
'C'est la vie.'

Bethan Jenkins (15) Penweddig School

SPRING

The sun rises early to brighten the sky,
The grass is all dewy, the light winds go by,
The flowers are blooming, the birds start to sing,
The winter's departed, the spring's settling in.

Winter sleepers rub their eyes,
A last good yawn before they rise,
Full of vigour they begin,
The happy days that make it spring.

Bare branches clothe again
Whilst birds are busy nesting.
The flowers bloom in various shades
The spring is now its fragrance stage.

Three months go by from March to June
Another season's gone,
The long hot Summer's turn has come
To sing its pretty song.

Frances Hebenstreit (15) Dyffryn Ogwen School

A SPELL TO CURE BOILS

All together:

S plish, splash:
P inch of pole cat;
E ar of elephant;
L ung of lion;
L iver of lynx;

T ongue of tiger;
O rifice of orang-u-tan;

C heek of cheetah;
U nicorn's urethra;
R ib of rat;
E ye of eagle

B rain of bat,
O il of octopus;
I ntestine of ibex;
L eg of lizard;
S creaming agony!

Catriona Duffy (12) St Gerard's School

CHRISTMAS TREE

Here proudly I stand
All the year round.
Growing, only to be cut down,
then to be planted in artificial ground.

I'll be prettily decorated
with tinsel and colours
and hide wrapped gifts
for all those others.

Charlotte Tivy-Jones (13) St Gerard's School

BUNGEE!

Waiting,
everything passing slowly,
green grass and pine tree's beauty turns ugly,
Uninterested laughter turns to unreachable sneers.

The monster's hand locks on me
lifts me against natural gravity
the view envelops me,
but I'm only aware of the distance to the ground,
She stops where she wants
I have no say,
She makes me feel stupid,
Adrenaline shoots through me with every pulse
like chilling oil, cooling on unnaturally hot
engine,
My body won't obey my petrified mind,
I drop.

I scream bungee! but it's muffled by the
hurtling air,
My throbbing body can feel the sly, sharp
pain electrocuting me,
it races up towards me,
making me breathless,
The thing I trusted grabs me,
and pulls me away from mortal life.
but then drops me again,
I must have a smile on my face
I feel great.

Michael Gardener (15) St Gerard's School

TEACHERS

Are teachers really people?
Do they really have a life?
Are they really someone's mother? brother?
Sister? husband? or wife?
I'm sure they're really robots,
Beamed down from the sky
To spy on teenage children
And swat them like a fly.
They take away our freedom and
any sign of fun,
And I've never seen a smiling one
anywhere under the sun.
They hand out lines and make up rules,
As if it were out of fashion,
But of course the ones from our school
are absolutely smash'!

Bethan Weedon (13) St Gerard's School

BONFIRE NIGHT

November the fifth comes once a year
To remember the treacherous guy
Who planned to blow the Government,
Way up into the sky.

Now he sits on a pile of fire,
Glowing, spitting flames bright.
Children coming the sight to admire,
Bringing laughter to the dismal night.

Oo's and aah's as the rockets rise,
Spreading colours through the skies,
Upturned faces smiling eyes,
Forgetting the dangers that could arise.

Burns and blisters,
To those who dare,
Enjoy themselves,
Without due care.

Sarah Williams (14) St Gerard's School

EXAMS

'Begin' I turn over the page.
I scribble my name at the top
I look over the first questions.
Not too hard, I suppose.
Maths! My worst subject.
All those weekends of study and revision,
All for this.
My hand clicks into action.
I pick up my pen but can't seem to write.
Uncomfortably in my seat I sit,
I look at the first sums again
Well I might as well have a go.

Once I have answered the first question,
The rest seem to follow easily.
It surprises me when I look at the clock,
There is only ten minutes to go.
I check over my work.
It seems to look fine to me.
Before I know it, the teacher calls. . .
'Time up!'
I hand in my paper.
It's all over!

Helen Coates (13) St Gerard's School

MURDER MOST HORRID

The room is silent,
a dagger appears,
the victim lies asleep,
Still no noise is made.

Then the slashing starts
the dagger plunges in,
and smoothly back out,
the victim lies in pain.

The blood is gushing out,
like a running hose pipe,
puddles of blood,
and footprints left by the murderer. . .

The victim is . . . *Dead!*

Sarah Hennessey (13) St Gerard's School

WAITING

I've been waiting for eternity
To see a star or cloud.
Watching the sand in Time's hourglass,
Only seeing my own shroud.

Seeing the smooth, cold wall of iron,
Fear in everyone's face.
Thinking, waiting, watching, hoping
In this Death inviting place.

Before, life never was so precious,
Or never the love of Man.
All this unfair imprisonment,
Just because one boy ran.

Phoebe Hale (13) St Gerard's School

ETERNITY

You were my hero
My voice,
My life.
You stood by me,
through peace,
through strife.

All my problems,
I could share,
You wanted to hear,
You wanted to care.

You held my hand,
as I walked on the wall.
Later you assured me
that boy would call.

You taught me,
to respect myself,
Worried if I was
not in good health.

Remember,
When I had,
had too much to drink,
You held my hair,
I threw up in the sink.

Days will go
days will come
You were
you are
always, my mum.

Erika Boe (15) St Gerard's School

SEA

The wind rocked her as she stood on the cliff,
Gently swaying her forwards. . . backwards
The cold heartless sea beat the rocks
relentlessly with its impatient waves,
Its salty fingers reaching up to grab her heart.
The icy rain beating down on her face.
The sea was slowly dragging her in,
A serpent enveloping its prey.

One step and she would be gone,
Away from the upset and torment of life,
Just one step. . .

The sea drew back from the towering cliff,
Smugly content with another victim.

Charlotte Handby (13) St Gerard's School

NO-ONE

The lonely sound of a creaking chair,
But there was no-one, no-one there.
The moon shone through the window panes,
Upon the lonely creaking chair,
But still there was no-one, no-one there.

The cracking of a twig under foot,
But there was no-one, no-one there,
The wind blew through the bare branched trees,
Across the mossy forest floor,
But still there was no-one, no-one there.

Elizabeth Boddington (13) St Gerard's School

THE SEA

The crystal shimmers on the water's face
Mediterranean green and blues
Vibrant colours full of grace
Whisper softly through the breeze.

The sea so calm at the edge of the bay
Swish, swish, swish, swish
Gently moving stones away
Swish, swish, swish, swish.

Rachel Bacon (14) St Gerard's School

YEARS FROM NOW

Years from now, way up high,
A terrible war will wage in the sky.
With lots of people down below
Sitting around to see the show
Watching lots of people die,
And listening to their families cry.
The planes are fast and well armed
The people on earth watch unharmed
As the planes shoot across the sky
More and more take off, and fly.
The good guys and the bad guys
Shoot each other in the skies.
While way down, down below,
More and more people watch the show.
Finally they run out of planes,
And decide to stop their silly games.
Many more now have died,
And many more families cried.
I pray the next century,
Will see a lot more hope for me.

Carol Young (13) St Gerard's School

THE STRAY CAT

Makes his move on his food for today
Once had a home, but now is a stray
He sat by the fire content and warm
But all that changed one frosty morn
He was thrown out of the car in a place, far away
Told not to come back another day
So now he has to find his feet
With only his skills to earn him his meat.

Nichola Raihani (14) St Gerard's School

ON THE BRINK . . .

Forehead furrowed, drenched in sweat,
Eyes screwed tight, afraid of the future.
Falling down a bottomless pit,
Life is dragging me further down.
Only one way to find the bottom . . .
I need to hear those words . . . but no-one speaks.
I can see the end;
Closer, closer, I'm nearly there.
Blood trickling, a river flowing,
A pathway . . .
My body is drained of life,
Life escaping almost free.

Your words are too late . . .
I no longer hear.

Kate Magee (14) St Gerard's School

THE DAWNING

The heavens have provoked her;
There's no turning back,
Enraged and tumultuous she explodes
Fearless and tyrannical, her power unequalled,
Exploiting our weaknesses in a patronising game.

Extreme upon her surface,
Merciless to all that dare confront her,
Full blooded and vigorous she tears through the bays,
She knows no bounds to her destruction.
Everything surrenders to her abuse.

At a distance we are mesmerised
By the swift white horses galloping at her beck and call,
Entranced by her sheer power
Amazed by the destruction left behind her.

The dawn has come.
Now there is silence.
Apart from a cat-like lapping of sea on sand.
All is as still as the death she created
A mirror image in the reflection of the sun's rays
Gulls, shadows against the fiery sun.
She waits.

Kate Wilkinson (14) St Gerard's School

LABORATORY TESTS

In a laboratory hidden away,
People work both night and day.
Working on chemicals that kill,
Lots of little bottles, that's what they fill.
Testing hairspray in rabbits' eyes,
They don't care that the rabbits can't cry.
But what if scientists became infected?
Are they chopped up and laboratory tested?

Katie Jenkins (13) St Gerard's School

FIELD IN GLOUCESTERSHIRE

A sudden beam of light
Brushes the field. The dewy ground
is unsettled by the steps of man.

Silence, a shovel strikes,
shushing and ringing sounds
of metal on soil and stone.

The breath of death evaporates.
Something has been heaved
into the field's gash.

Everything has changed:
The field is scared,
The wind moans scornfully.

Laura Owen (14) St Gerard's School

EMOTIONS

A twisted turmoil of emotion,
Caged in a web of pain.
My heart is congealing.
Hot arms constricting my breath, my movement
tightening round my body
restricting emotions from flowing.
They cramp, my body rages for air,
                                        for love,
                                        to speak,
                            to be understood.
          I scream
          No-one hears.
Fingers enclose my throat
A panic suffocates my body.

I burst free, like a taut spring released,
My body exhilarated by the torture.
Every pore gasping for air.
I'm free, I can do anything I want to.
My emotions overflow, they bathe in an oasis
not grasping the concept of being allowed to explore.
My mind tries to understand, to sort things out.
My hand flows across the paper,
thoughts tripping over the pen.

Everything seems clearer now,
Calm descends on my body.
I feel soothed,
the terror of yesterday is smothered by this
blanket of understanding.

Marie-Anne Witcombe (15) St Gerard's School

THE WIND

The wind is a wild wolf,
howling in the dark night,
its sharp claws scratch at the windows and door,
frightening everything that hears it.

The breeze is a mother wolf,
nurturing its young,
playing gently in the bushes,
calmly watching over them.

The gale is the hungry wolf,
Pursuing its prey,
it cruelly rips up its catch,
salivating excessively in anticipation.

Richard Waterton (13) St Gerard's School

WRINKLED SHORE

The sea splashes down on the wrinkled shore,
The rock pools are flooded by galloping waves,
Crabs burrow down, the seaweed scatters.

The sound of the seagulls, like screaming cats,
Searching for food in the ferocious rows of the waves.
The sound of the sea,
The taste of the salt,
The sand that hits you like bullets.

The sea-anemones huddled against the rocks.
The crabs buried themselves down.

Melanie Burroughs (12) St Gerard's School

CONKERS

When I was just a boy of eight,
Percy Prachett, my best mate,
Had a collection of conkers, large and small
He'd played many people and beat them all.

Then one dark day I went to play,
I'd found a conker on the way.
I bought a shoelace to tie it to,
Then we started playing at ten past two.

By four o'clock we had to stop,
Percy Prachett was no longer top,
All of his conkers had been broken,
He asked me where I'd found my token.

I took him to my secret place,
Oh dear! You should have seen his face,
Thousands of conkers lay on the floor,
More than we'd ever seen before.

Josephine Connolly (14) St Gerard's School

FASCINATION

The water in the shallow rock pool gleamed in the warm summer's sun,
Full of fresh green seaweed, shells and sea anemones
Left by the sea, after a high tide.
Just waiting to be taken by small children.

The slight aroma of the salty sea, and the gentle sound of the
peaceful waters
Now seem miles away from me,
As I am engrossed by the fascinating beautiful rock pool,
Laden with wildlife to please the eye of the beholder.

Richard Finch (11) St Gerard's School

NOT JUST A SHOWER

Waves like hands,
Dropping seaweed on the shore,
Chocolate wrappers, marks in the sand,
Telling of crowds there a while ago.

The air feels heavy,
Thunder, maybe lightning to come?
Squawking seagulls, searching, looking,
For cover from the approaching storm.

Storm is here
Not just a shower,
The rain is tipping, pouring down,
Leaves the shore an ugly place.

Next day brings the sun,
With crowds surely on their way;
Divers, swimmers, bathers, builders,
Soon to be a bustling beach.

Gareth Jones (12) St Gerard's School

MOONLIGHT DANCE

Seaweed like weak, wrinkled hands glimmered in the moonlight of the evening
Crabs scuttled sideways along the bottom of the rock pool, like soldiers at war.
Salt hit the jagged rocks' edge, carried by the wind.
Sea anemones, all colours, fled for safety, like mice when a cat pounces.
Air tasting like bitter mackerel.
Icy, overlapping water, touched my hands as they plunged in the moonlight pool.
Water smelling like moules, garlic and herbs, all in boiling water.
Ripple pranced over ripples like sea horses, wild with excitement.
The moonlight dance began.

Rhiannon Jones (12) St Gerard's School

A DISFIGURED BEACH

What was once a beach with joy and laughter,
Is now a beach with no life at all.
Seagulls have disappeared. People have gone home,
And all that is left is litter and darkness.

Crisp packets and cigarettes boxes are discarded,
Clumps of seaweed lie all around.
Shells that were once pearly white,
Are now pieces that have been stamped on.

Not a boat on the horizon,
Not a sound at all.
A beach that was once alive,
Is now a deserted, disfigured one.

Emma Verghese (12) St Gerard's School

THE RELENTLESS SEA

The wind roars like a great tiger
Over the dusty sands, blowing and bellowing
Lifeless and lonely.
Deserted and quiet lies the beach.
The salty sea smell,
The stinging pain of sand against my legs.
The gritty taste and feel of sand in my face.
The clanging and crashing of ships' booms against the mast.
The sea relentlessly pounds the rocks.
As if some great invisible hammer were being thrust against them.

James Williams (12) St Gerard's School

ROLLERCOASTER!

In the distance,
I hear the roar,
The piercing screams,
Echoing through my mind.
Like wind over a desert.
I'm surely too young to die,
Holy smoke, I'm gonna cry.
The roar again.
That roar again.
Adrenaline pumps through my mind and body
The pain. No!
My legs shake,
My mind seizes,
My stomach churns,
My heart stops.
Am I dead? Please?
No. It's not as easy as that.
I sit down.
I'm strapped in.
As we start
I'm no longer in control of myself.
If I find myself joining the pathetic chorus of screams.
Here comes the loop.
I'm dead. I'm dead.
Upside down, weightlessness,
heaven.
I wanna do it again.
Yes!
The rollercoaster stops.
My heart starts again.
Was all that pain and anguish worth it?
No way!
Move! I'm gonna be sick.

John Gardener (13) St Gerard's School

FORGOTTEN

Like so many dancing devils,
The blowing litter prances.
The beach seems sad and lonely,
As the waves crash in and out.
The bleached, boarded house,
The stranded seaweed,
The one-way footprints,
Never coming back.
Someone's forgotten glove,
And a yellowed newspaper.
Faded colours.
Grey, ghostly,
Grey, drab,
Grey, dismal,
Grey, lonely.
The solitary seagull soars and cries.

Catherine Field (12) St Gerard's School

MY BEACII

The rough sand glides over the beach
Like a swarm of wasps which hits you like a whip.
The salty waves crash against the rocks
With the spray that falls on you like snow.
The icy cold water splashes against your feet
And the cold anticipation of numbness hits you.
The leaves have covered the beach
And the geese ahead herald the coming of autumn.

Stephanie Parry (12) St Gerard's School

TRANSFORMATION

Early evening.
The deserted beach lies dormant,
The tide gently rolls up the beach,
Like a strange blue carpet,
Making attractive impressions in the sand.
The long grass in the dunes,
Sways gracefully in the cool breeze,
As a seagull swoops down onto a slippery, wet rock,
Gazing into a clear, shimmering rock pool -
Searching for his prey.
Then off he goes again,
His outstretched body leaning towards the sun,
Rising into the multi-coloured sky,
Wings flapping, gliding and rising,
His cry echoes for miles around.
Clouds start rolling swiftly across the sky,
Rushing, darting, quicker and quicker.
A low rumbling can be heard,
The ground trembling in the distance
The sea becomes aggressive, slashing at a cliff,
Sending a shower of foam into the air,
Descending back into the sea,
Creating ripples dancing across the icy water.
Soon the sky can take no more,
As salty drops of rain hit my face,
And the wind blows a thousand grains of sand -
Across the beach - like a sandstorm in a desert.

Sharita Oomeer (12) St Gerard's School

NIGHT CHILDREN

When we go into the glen
Let us go alone.
To hear the whispered secrets of the trees
Of ancient stories told.
The trees do stand around us
Watchguards thru' the night
Keep us safe from others, their ever calming might.

The silent moon above us
A torch light through the dark.
We dance amongst her moonbeams,
We hide between the trees.
Sip the cool clear liquid
And wish our dreams come true.

Night creatures do not fear us
For we ourselves are one.
No longer mortal beings
But spirits free to roam.
Our love could light the forest
The shining thru' the gloom.
We'll dance together till daybreak
Seen only by the moon

Fay Josephy (17) St Gerard's School

THE PARK

Children playing; trees swaying,
Ladies talking, ducks squawking
Bins overflowing with litter; raindrops pitter.
Robins singing; church bells ringing;
Green grass; swings moving fast;
Sun no longer bright; it's nearly tonight.

Park's bare.

Kelly Wright (14) St Gerard's School

EVERYTHING TO LOSE

'Go on, take it,
Have a try
It's really fine,
We wouldn't lie.
It'll make you feel good,
Make you feel high,
Well it would -
If you'd try.
Just the once,
Won't do no harm,
Come on,
Can't we twist your arm?
We all do it,
Why can't you?
Are you a freak?
Not scared are you?
Don't believe what's on the news,
Come on now,
What's there to lose?
Don't you want to feel real good?
Go on, try it,
You know you should.'

Clare Screeton (15) St Gerard's School

BEACH SEARCH

Ignored, she walks on to the overcrowded beach.
She stops, stares, looks around,
She walks on, exasperated.
She dodges, she swerves, she searches.
She jumps, she ducks, still searching,
Searching for peace, searching for tranquillity.

She looks around oppressed, sighs a doubtful sigh,
'Bingo!' she mutters as she rushes towards it,
The emptiness is soon filled by a relieved family.
She turns around slowly,
Another place! . . . She gathers her wits,
Disappointment as it's filled by selfish cricketers.

Then she spots it, the top of the sand dune,
She looks around, wishing, hoping.
No other arrows aimed at the target,
She pulls back, aims and lets fly,
She arrives watching the last places being filled up.
She lies down. Peace at last.

Eli Nickson (12) St Gerard's School

THE ROCKET GIRL

There was a girl, now she does lie
under the black, eternal sky.
She watched the fireworks bang and hiss
each blowing the moon a farewell kiss.
She gazed enthralled, all full of wonder
Wishing she could fly like thunder.
She whirled around, took a rocket
far too big to fit in her pocket,
With cord and string she tied it to herself
and crept away with practised stealth.
She lit the fuse, smiled, too late now
and gave a final graceful bow.
But fireworks die, as did she
Such colour is not immortality.

Hawys Pritchard Jones (14) St Gerard's School

MOTOR BIKE

Heart thumping,
Foot tense,
On the kick start,
Ready to go,
Engine roaring,
Lights go green,
Winning is my dream,
Lungs dry,
Gasping for air,
Hunching forwards,
Angle turn,
Knuckles white on the throttle,
Adrenalin pumping,
Flag in the dust,
Over the line,
I have won.
Wheelie!

Rupert Cunliffe (12) St Gerard's School

WAITING FOR DAWN

The crescent moon had dwindled
From a night of storm and wind.
Gingerly, the light shone down
Onto a beach which nurtured peace.

Glistening, the gentle waves
Leapt upon the sleeping sand.
Spray arose against the rocks
As they lay lifeless, undisturbed.

The shells retreated hastily
As the waves intensified;
Their all persuasive power
Hurling the innocent shells away.

A million priceless pebbles
Saluted the entrancing scene;
The seagulls glided gracefully,
Watching and waiting for dawn.

Tanya Hubbard (13) St Gerard's School

WAR

I glance over my shoulder,
And see her standing there.
A small and dirty sunken face,
Surrounded by scruffy black hair.

Somewhere nearby: another explosion,
As horror mounts in this ongoing fight.
But not even a shiver, a shudder,
Comes from this body so shaken by plight.

Her family are dead, all relations lost,
But she lives on in this nightmare; her life.
her life which was once carefree fun,
Is now rubble, starvation and strife.

In her mind she screams out in pain,
Trying hard to let the world know.
But to us, her small voice is lost,
In the noise of our own private lives.

Jessica Henderson (13) Ysgol Eifionydd

AMMONITE STONE

Cracked egg
Broken open
Dinosaur born
Terrifying, made,
Hurting people.
Running after them.
Escaping back in time.
200 years ago.

Jamie Stonehouse (12) Ysgol John Bright

WAR!

As dawn came,
I surveyed the mess,
Desolate marsh land
Hung with stress,
The breeze strong and heavy,
Brought cries of pain,
War balance on two shoulders,
The nation's strain
'My son fights for the country'
I heard a mother's voice.
'Yea I fights for England,
but that was her choice!'
I left a perfect life-style,
to enter pain and strife,
And now amongst the rubble
I'm fighting for my life.

Laura Gorst (12) Ysgol John Bright

THE TURQUOISE EYE OF THE WIND

These colourful strands of feathers
Are blue green yellow and brown
This *peacock* who wore these
Should be very proud

The feathers remind me of gentle wind
The spots are eyes watching you
Every move you make
It walks around slowly and haughtily

Jonathan Hughes (11) Ysgol John Bright

FIREWORKS' DAY

Snap, crack, bang, fizz!
Up go the sparklers,
Up with a whizz,
All of the rockets, screaming around
Oh my ears! What a terrible sound.
The fire is snapping,
The children are clapping,
The fire's alight
On Bonfire Night!

But then it rains,
It always rains,
Everyone goes home,
Sulking and moaning,
And generally whinging,
About how the council,
Could have picked a finer night!

But then there's a few,
Who decide to stay,
And watch the flames,
Just fizzle away,
In a turmoil of colour,
Red, black and grey.
Because it's always the same,
On Fireworks' Day.

David Robinson (14) Ysgol John Bright

A LIFELESS OBJECT

Hollow, lifeless, strange and lonely,
Fragile, oddly shaped and cold.
Once lived its life, but now is cracked,
Patterned, deserted, unusual and old.

Plain looking, smooth, but solid,
Empty, delicate and quite hard.
Oddly shaped, deceased and sharp,
Maybe found in someone's back yard.

Jonathan Davies (11) Ysgol John Bright

AN INDIAN DOLL

Soft and hard.
An old Indian made of cotton,
It smells old.
The inside is made of wood,
Lines of strings,
It's light in a way,
She looks happy,
Wearing ragged clothes,
Her arms are birds' claws,
The colours are fading
The hands and feet are twigs,
The baby is wrapped in an old musty ragged cloth.
The red eyes show that she is tired.

Michael Gwynne (11) Ysgol John Bright

MINER'S MATCHBOX

Light spooky feathery shiny
Swinging on his belt down the mine
Strike, the match is lit
Jack Griffiths down the mine at
ten years old
Dark damp wet and cold
Jack Griffiths soaked to the bone
Home, home after a hard day's work
Jack Griffiths sat at the table
tired eyes looking round
Next day and Jack's at work
digging for all he is worth.

Ben Hodgkinson (11) Ysgol John Bright

THE CLOUD OF ROCK

Hard and heavy,
A stony staircase pointing to infinity,
Chipped and worn
A cloud of rock rests for millions of years.

The ancient snail lies dormant
Hidden from all the world.
Its stony exterior
Protecting its fragile existence.

Danny Wagstaff (12) Ysgol John Bright

AUTUMN'S COLD

Chilly wind, blowing trees,
Falling leaves
Bright colours dancing in the air,
As trees and bushes turn slowly bare.

Cold weather freezes rivers and ponds,
Losing all of summer's songs,
And as nuts and berries begin to ripen,
Cold weather's grasp begins to tighten.

No more sunshine only rain,
That patters on the window pane.
Shorter days and longer nights
As autumn's wind finally bites.

Lindsey Trafford (13) Ysgol John Bright

THE DANCING BRANCH

It snapped when it was young
A sudden gust threw it down
it lay quiet, still and dead . . .
hid its living core.
Its gnarled and knotted shape
was a man dancing his last chance.

Now the same wind whispers its
message of hope
And the sea wraps its arms
around the dancer.
Meanwhile the golden sun rises majestically
and waits for the day
When he can dance again.

Ceri Brown (11) Ysgol John Bright

THE CRYSTAL

A whirlpool as clean as an
eye,
Like a star in the galaxy
sky,
Back to earth as a comet;
it's found
Hundreds of years later
to be a stone
In the countryside.

Craig Phillips (12) Ysgol John Bright

THE DRIFTWOOD MEMORIES

Stormy night, lightning strikes,
Forests fall into the sea,
Trees smash onto the rocks
Into a million pieces,
They part to go their own way.

The next day on the beach,
People find some wood,
One single piece, all by itself,
Taken home,
It looks like a dancer,
Dancing forever.

Smooth to touch
With bumps on it here and there,
Picked up and treasured forever,
An odd shaped piece of wood.

Caroline Edwards Hughes (11) Ysgol John Bright

DYING DRIFTWOOD

Old and forgotten, crying in its spirit,
Growing no longer, a loss of life,
Brown, grey, dull, bright no more,
Peaceful, contented, resting for ever more.

Discovered on the washed up shore,
Tugged, worn by the frantic frightening sea,
Engraving weird patterns on its crumbly old cover,
Pushed and shoved by gigantic waves.

This skeleton was once a beautiful tree,
Now dry, dead and motionless,
This solid texture slowly fading away,
Struck by nature still living.

Helen Nesbitt (12) Ysgol John Bright

THE DRIFTING SEAHORSE

The seahorse,
Dead and ancient,
Washed away and drifting
In the calm, blue green water.
Its lonely soul shall never,
Return to the world.
Yellow, and grey from dirt.
Rough and spiky.
Washed up on a beach,
But special and kept,
in a rusty old tin.

Sally Nesbitt (12) Ysgol John Bright

THE FOSSIL

Hard
Spiral
Rough
Very old.
Ancient animal
Trapped in rock.
Stone prisoner,
Creature of the sea,
History lesson for us.

Peter Drake (11) Ysgol John Bright

THE MATCHBOX

It's shiny and golden in colour
A bit of rust on it
But it did not matter.
The head is like a comb
And the beak is like a sharp razor.
It was always in the mine.
It was dark
So it had to be shiny and clean.
It gave the owner a light when he was scared
when he needed it for his candle
on his helmet.
It had to be rough so he could feel it in the dark
There was a hole in the bottom so he could feel
it in the dark
It was light so it was not heavy on his belt.

David Ellis (11) Ysgol John Bright

WHO NEEDS TEENAGERS?

Teenagers, who needs them?
We all need teenagers.
Without teenagers
What would we do?
Just think if teenagers were
Not invented
Who would we shout
And scream at?
The police wouldn't have
A job.
Spot cream companies
Would have no business.
B T wouldn't be able
To present parents with a
Big bill.
Teenagers day dream in
Class.
Talk to their friends
'What's on at the weekend?'

Teenagers
          Who needs them?

Anthony Jones (13) Ysgol John Bright

THE FAN

the Fan is different colours
like green silver and blue
Turquoise brown it is soft
smooth it rustles like trees

Nicola Geale (11) Ysgol John Bright

A CHAIN OF MEMORIES

Heavy and stiff
it can't move or flow,
rusted knots clamped together.

Yellow and brown
black and white
cracks and dents

It pulled big ships
to the bottom of the sea,
it's solid, frozen
ugly and knobbly,
a bony finger
pointing.

Stephanie Gaines (12) Ysgol John Bright

THE GEODYNE

An alien's egg
From out of space,
With cracks as if
It is going to hatch.
A fearsome alien
Emerges and liquids
Ooze from its mouth.

Inside the egg
Are colours that
Nobody's seen before.
Deep in the egg is a labyrinth
that nobody comes out of.

Carl Richardson (11) Ysgol John Bright

DON'T

If you want detention,
Or a slap across the face,
Just ask Mrs Evans and she'll put you in your place,
So don't run along the corridor,
Stuff gum into your face,
Tie your tie around your waist,
Or you'll be in disgrace,

Don't be cheeky to the teachers,
Or smoke behind the hall,
Don't wear your shirt outside your skirt,
Or you'll be for it all.

Don't leave knickers on the floor,
Or stuff your ciggies in the drawer,
Blast your eardrums with Take That,
Or spill your shandy on the mat!
Don't hog the bathroom all the time,
Or keep your boyfriend on the line,
Hid Granny's teeth in the butter,
and laugh when she can only mutter.

Don't pinch your best friend's boyfriend,
Or lock her in the loo,
Tell her mum and dad she's boozing,
At Broadway until two.
Don't tell her that she's gweni
Or her face is one big spot,
That she looks like Mrs Blobby,
And is the school prize swot.

Elinor Griffith (11) Ysgol John Bright

THE TIGER

Like a tiger lying on a beach
Helpless and slowly into the sand
Moving from side to side.
Waiting, just waiting for someone to pick him up
And save him from the sea
And from getting drowned
As just in the nick of time
Someone picked him up
And took him home.

Rae Williams (11) Ysgol John Bright

LISTEN!

Wet, cold and covered
From head to toe, are
Men dragging themselves
Helplessly through the snow.
Limbs missing,
And eyes lost -
They'll never know what'll happen next.
Gassed victims give a loud harsh cough,
And dozens break their necks.

For those who don't know
What this is about,
I'll tell you now.
Listen: men dying,
Suffering pain.
In the First World War
There was nothing to gain.

John Witter (15) Ysgol John Bright

THE MATCHBOX

It's smooth and rough and sharp
It look like leaves on the top of his head.
The candle on his helmet
And the match was his hope
to make the boy feel brave.

Adam Thomas (12) Ysgol John Bright

THE PARK

They say we're loud and most uncouth,
But we're a prime example of modern youth.
We sit, some smoke,
We laugh and chat
But we don't look for trouble
We're not like that!
We go to the park
'Cos there's nowhere to go.
We've asked for a Youth Club
But the answer was no!
The police come here hourly
To check things are right
But we see them coming
With their flashing blue lights.
It's the oldies who call them
The ones with the dogs.
They've ruined our soccer pitch.
It stinks like the bogs.
As long as we live here
We'll go to the park
For now it's our hangout
For when it gets dark.

David Shimmin (16) Ysgol John Bright

AUTUMN

*A*ged is the year. The year is nearly dead.
*U*nco-ordinated golden and brown leaves will fall.
*T*hinking of a long, harsh winter ahead.
*U*nderneath the autumn cloud.
*M*igrating swallows call out aloud
*N*ovember's on the way. I dread to see another day.

Jonathan Alexander (13) Ysgol John Bright

WAR

Among the sludge inside my hole,
My heart cried out in pain,
For lying beside me cold and still,
Was my friend who died in vain.

The bullet came from nowhere,
And pierced him like a dart.
He fell to the floor, dying
And his cries drummed through my heart.

I sat there staring, staring,
What else could I do?
Why him, not me? I asked myself
I wished I'd died too.

No explanation for his death,
No reason I could find,
Apart from the greed and selfishness,
Of creatures called *mankind*.

And all the memories of that war,
Haunt my tortured mind.
And although I'm safe and home at last,
I can't leave those thoughts behind.

Kate Lennard (16) Ysgol John Bright

LEAVES

L eathery boots with melting frost.
E very fish is not going to be lost.
A fter the floods the salmon run.
V arious fish leap the falls.
E very day which hardly lasts,
S ilvery fish starts spawning fast.

David Carl Adshead (13) Ysgol John Bright

AFRAID, ALONE

If I was afraid, all alone,
Who would I turn to?
I'd lay in my bed,
My parents are dead,
I keep praying, what can I do?

My brothers and sisters hate me,
My aunty and uncle don't care.
My dog called Ben,
Is at the age of ten.
When he dies I've got nobody spare.

I've got no money, running out
Nothing at all to wear
My nain has died
So has my taid,
Nobody to turn to, no-one cares.

There's only one who cares
This is my imaginary friend
My friend called Billy
You may find silly,
Is with me until the end.

Mathew Williams (12) Ysgol John Bright

SCHOOL

I wake up in the morning,
Fall out of bed,
Get dressed, fall down the stairs,
And bump my head.
Take a coffee to Mum,
I burn my hand,
Tread on a cat on my paper round.
I go and meet my mates,
Paul, Chris and Ben,
Anthony's clucking like a demented hen.
The bell goes,
It's registration,
Someone's late, Mr Sharrad's mad,
He needs resuscitation.
We head to our lesson,
As the second bell goes,
Is it mathematics,
Yes it is.
Oh No.
Maths wasn't too bad,
But now it gets worse,
It's the dread historical
Real Welsh curse.
Next it's science,
Then P E ,
Now to the station,
And home for tea.

David Waddington (11) Ysgol John Bright

MY PRIMARY SCHOOL

Bus is here! 'Bye Mum, bye Dad,'
Into the bus I go.
Next, pick up Gaz and Cheryl
And Danny; Oh! He's so slow!

Pick up Leon (the awful pain)
Aled and Michael (he's late again!)
Turn around in the spooky quarry,
Mustn't be late, Hurry! Hurry!

Past the Queen's Head,
Have pint or three,
Into the school, and,
Crash into the tree.

Walk down the stairs,
See all your friends,
But you can't wait
Till school ends!

Bell rings;
It's assembly time.
We could do without
The singing and the rhymes.

Bell goes again:
Oh no! Now Welsh!
Prefer to do Art,
Or English, or Belch!

Teachers are one thing
We'd do without.
They never talk properly:
They always shout!

Caroline Jones (12) Ysgol John Bright

DISILLUSION

The emptiness creeps up
And wraps itself around me
I feel so weak and helpless
And no-one else can see.

Death took her away with it o o o
In the darkness of the night
It came without me realising
There was nothing I could do to fight

If only she had gone in an instant
And been run over by the bus
After the false hope, that transfusion
Only took her away from us.

All the helpless waiting
She lived on borrowed time
In the end the illness lingered
And I knew she was going to die.

Now I only have memories
Of what we together once had
I want to remember the good times
But bury forever the bad.

She was always the quiet one
Often in a dream
I gave her the push that she needed
Together we were a team

What would you honestly think of her,
If you knew she died of AIDS
You'd think she was a sleaze or a junkie,
That's how the disease is portrayed.

Bethany Bennett (12) Ysgol John Bright

DON'T

Don't steal your mum's lipstick
or take your dad's Prittstick.
Don't play on your brother's Sega
or you'll be in danger.
Don't ever over feed the fishes
or you'll have to do the dishes.
Don't stand on the cat for she might
bite back.
Always do your homework and never
chew gum.
Never smoke behind the shed
or else you will get done.
Don't pull your teacher's skirt up
and show her gaudy bloomers!
Do your tables every night
and never wear your Puma's.

Kay Ellen Morris (11) Ysgol John Bright

TEENAGER

Then the teenager always in a fight
Fooling around at night
Scaring grannies in town
Don't smile just frown
Vandalising the walls
Shop windows and doors
Eating junk food
Weird language
Chill out
Yo dude
Never go to school
What a fool

Carl Jones (13) Ysgol John Bright

A TEENAGER'S LIFE

Tots we were, teens we are,
Ridiculous hair styles!
Outrageous clothes.

Dancing! And raving! Parties too,
Smoking! And drinking! That's bad for you.

Mum says,
'All you do is sit around
I clean your rooms. Babysit. I don't get paid!'

Your mum and dad take you to school
Embarrass you by saying,
'Tuck your vest in'
Or something like that.

It's hard being a teenager
Being told what to do.

Zoe Robertson (13) Ysgol John Bright

IT'S HARD BEING A TEENAGER

It's hard being a teenager, you know,
And your parents just don't understand.
They shout and they bawl,
They scream and they call
Tell you, 'It's a stage you're going through.'
They tell your room must be spotlessly clean,
You've got to be home by ten,
Visit your grandma on Sundays,
Who to go out with and when.
Make sure your homework is finished
And never get in the way.
Take the dog for its morning walk
Then say, you do nothing all day.

It's hard being a teenager, you know
Being told you're always wrong,
Then one day you're eventually right,
They tell you your nose is too long.
The radio's always too loud,
The phone bill is just too high,
You always eat all the food up,
And parents don't understand why.
It is your fault your sister's screaming,
You try to help, you're told to go.
They tell you're just adolescent
It's hard being a teenager, you know.

Gemma Haslam (13) Ysgol John Bright

MISSING PART

Teenager! Vandal! Hooligans!
Disgrace to the society.
That's what old people think of teenagers.
Teenagers! They really hit the *jackpot* with teachers.
Teachers think we're evil.
Parents like teenagers.
Someone to go on errands.
Always nice when they want something.
First they ask
If not successful
They *order!*
This isn't fair
We are human
Human.
We're just like anyone else
Being a teenager isn't easy.

Tommy Walker (13) Ysgol John Bright

A PLEASANT TEENAGER

I'm a teenager,
A very pleasant one in fact,
People make me out to be a hooligan
What do they know?
They don't know about teenagers,
They're too old fashioned,
We like watching TV
And listening to tapes.
They think we like listening
To *classical music*,
They treat us like children.
What next?
Last Christmas
Opening my first present
And what was it?
A Postman Pat quilt.
I mean.
What could I say?
Oh thanks Mrs Thomas
It's really thoughtful of you.
I'll put it in the bin.
I mean
On my bed, straight away.
See.
I told you I was a
Pleasant lad.

Philip A Kendall (13) Ysgol John Bright

TEENAGERS!

You mustn't throw things on the ground
You mustn't put music on loud
That's what elders always say
You mustn't do this
You mustn't do that
But what about them?
They were never angels
Were they?
Even though they make us believe
They were.

Walking in town
Elderly people think
Just because we are younger
Than them
We will go around them.
I don't want
To do that anymore.
Then they think
We are horrible because
We don't always smile.

Carly Saville (13) Ysgol John Bright

JUST TYPICAL

Turn that music down!
It's down!
Tidy your room!
It's tidy!
Do your homework!
It's done!
Moan, mither, grumble,
Is that all you can do?

I've done lasagne for tea,
Don't like it!
You liked it this morning,
I didn't!
Fine, don't have anything!
Starve me!
Moan, mither, grumble,
Is that all you can do?
I've had enough of that,
And I've had enough of you!

Victoria Sarah Reynolds (13) Ysgol John Bright

THE TEENAGERS

T he teenager is when we're thirteen years of age.
H oping to leave school, as soon as possible.
E ven if there was a free lesson every day.

T eenagers start to graffiti on walls.
E ven if told not to.
E mpty pockets after the arcade.
N owadays teenagers smoke.
A ll teenagers start to do as they like.
G oing to shops and discos.
E agerly wanting more money.
R elaxing all the time.
S itting around.

Anthony So (13) Ysgol John Bright

IF AUTUMN WERE A PERSON

If autumn were a person
He'd be grumpy and miserable
And walk around sneezing on people
And killing plants and insects
He'd wear a brown jacket and
Trousers with holes in them
He'd also have a stick with which
To hit people
And a briefcase full of frost
At night he'd creep around the
Town, scattering frost and
Blowing cold winds
Never being seen and never
Being heard.
And then time will come when
He has to hand over reluctantly to winter
And disappear till next year.

Daniel Kirkham (13) Ysgol John Bright

AUTUMN DAYS

The seasons turn to autumn,
The year is getting older.
Nuts and berries ripen
And the air is getting colder.

In the mornings we see frost,
The day's weather's always rain.
The nights are coming earlier,
And then school starts again.

People sweep up fallen leaves
Their piles are getting higher.
They'll add the garden clippings
And have a good bonfire.

The colours of the autumn,
Red, orange, yellow and brown,
Aren't noticed because people
Walk with their heads down.

People gather fruit and nuts,
And make blackberry pies.
And, as the weather gets colder,
The autumn slowly dies.

Donna Harris (13) Ysgol John Bright

THE TEENAGER - AN OLD PERSON'S VIEW

I took a glance across the street,
Back came a giant stare.
There stood a teenager with smelly feet
And a head of radical hair.

Smashing windows that's their job,
Stealing from the shops.
None of their friends will snitch or dob.
Until one of us calls the cops.

Their hobby's staying out till crack of dawn.
Going to raves. Getting drunk.
Their clothes ripped and torn.
They smell like skunks.
I wasn't like that.
I think.

Rachel-Nichola Jones (13) Ysgol John Bright

A TYPICAL TEENAGER

When I was a teenager -
I respected my elders,
I was polite,
I tidied my room,
I did well in school,
I obeyed my parents. Came in when I was told.

Nowadays teenagers are -
Cheeky hooligans,
Who swear at us elders,
Who never tidy their rooms,
Who fight with their brothers and sisters,
Who never do as they are told.

When I was a teenager -
I went to Sunday school,
I never drew on walls,
I helped look after my brothers and sisters,
I never smoked or drank.

Nowadays teenagers are -
Like the Devil's children - doing wicked deeds,
Like graffitying on walls,
Like picking on their brothers and sisters,
Like staying out late,
Like smoking and drinking and who knows what else!

Times have changed since,
I was a teenager.

Suraya Bashar (13) Ysgol John Bright

I HATE THEM!

T hey're rude, lazy, very unhelpful,
E ven if you ask them, can't be bothered.
E very night on the phone for ages,
N o-one was allowed to do that in my day.
A t town on skateboards, dodging the grannies,
G alavanting around the shops - more CDs.
E venings of loud music issuing from their rooms,
R ude and ungrateful! Nothing like me.
Or
Are
They?

Kathleen Pritchard (13) Ysgol John Bright

AUTUMN

A utumn is rust, red, orange, gold and brown.
U p in the trees
T he coloured leaves are falling.
U nder and around the trees there is a
M ulti-coloured carpet, crunching beneath your feet.
N uts and fruits are ripening, ready for us to eat.

A utumn is black, brown, grey and beige.
U p in the trees
T he branches are dull and bare.
U nder and around the trees there is a
M uddy carpet of soggy, wet brown leaves.
N uts and fruit, over ripe, lie rotting on the ground.

Annabel Smith (13) Ysgol John Bright

TYPICAL TEENAGERS

Now I'm thirteen,
Adults think that I smoke and take drinks,
That I'm up to no good,
That I'm moody,
Bad tempered,
A young mini thug,
When I get in my parents say,
'Where've you been?
What have you been up to?'
I look at them,
And shrug.

Adam Jenkins (13) Ysgol John Bright

AUTUMN'S DECAY

Summer begins his yearly decay.
Coldness and gloom take over warm mornings.
Gold sun fades, grey mists take its place,
Robes of frost glaze each road.

Swaying trees shed their skins.
Piles of leaves descend to a sludge,
Heating bills rise as people stay indoors.
Only the faithful few brave the rain.

Nights become darker earlier now.
The wind whistles in the chimneys.
Hoards of cattle-like coaches,
Ferry the old to bingo.

Everything is dull and boring.
Wind blows off the slates of houses,
Everything closes early.
Autumn is in his downhill slalom.

Samantha Bridge (13) Ysgol John Bright

BLACK

Black is the colour of shiny coal,
Black is the colour of a tiny little mole,
Black is the colour of an eye after a fight,
Black is the colour of the sky at night,
Black magic puts curses on you,
Black cows eat grass and go *moo!*
Black people have the same rights as us,
Black taxis zoom past a bus.

James Andrew Parker (11) Brecon High School

THE STORM

I love to listen to the storm,
When I'm in bed all safe and warm,
I hear the rain and wind up high,
And the thunder in the sky,
The lightning is so sharp and bright,
It pokes its fingers through the night,
The wind is ringing loud and clear,
But, to me it is no fear

And all the sailors in the sea
Will all be wishing that they were me,
Cosy and warm at this time
On the night of the fierce storm.

Jemma Smith (11) Brecon High School

MY DRAGON

My dragon guards all my treasure,
My dragon watches me.
My dragon shows his teeth sometimes,
When I am looking after a flea.

My dragon has claws on his tail,
He has claws on his hands and feet.
His wings spread out, when he jumps about.
I've got to duck, look at the clock,
To see if it's time for tea.

When mum says, 'Tea's ready,'
My dragon and I walk steady.
First we start jogging, then we start running.
And get squashed in the door because of his *big* belly.

I get in first,
He gets in second.
We both call mum,
But she's on her bum,
Sucking her thumb.

I love my dragon,
And he loves me.
When he breathes fire,
On a tree,
It makes me feel cosy.

Amanda Winston (11) Brecon High School

THE STORM

The wind was howling down the chimney,
The wind was rattling at the doors,
The wind was racing down the garden path,
The wind was groaning at the windows,
Booming! Banging!
Booming! Banging!
The lightning's turning the sky bright amber,
The lightning's creeping through the sky,
The lightning's scaring faces at the windows,
The lightning's dodging through the clouds,
Booming! Banging!
Booming! Banging!

Joanne Hughes (12) Brecon High School

THE STORM

The wind is blowing, howling, whistling, rattling.
The clouds are scurrying across the sky.
Lightning strikes, bright, sharp, light.
It starts to rain big heavy drops.
Thunder rumbles very loudly.
Animals run and cower in their homes
People run and take shelter.
Frightened children cry.
Then the wind slows to a steady blow.
The clouds stop scurrying.
Lightning stops.
The thunder stops rumbling.
And the rain slows down to a drizzle.
Then the sun comes out, and a rainbow appears.
And everything is calm again.

Ryan John Richard Price (12) Brecon High School

MOUSE

I knew a mouse with a long tail,
Who ate a piece of cheese that was stale,
He had very long whiskers,
And he lived with his brothers and sisters,
By day in his nest he stayed,
And with his brothers and sisters he played,
He crept about the house at night,
Looking for food until first light,
One day whilst resting in a hat,
He was spotted by the old Tom cat,
A chase then followed,
The mouse was swallowed,
And that was the end of that.

Anne-Marie Evans (12) Brecon High School

THE STORM

Calm and quiet, the sky is clear,
The wind's picking up,
Maybe a storm is near.

The clouds creep over,
Like a cat on its prey.
It's getting quite cold now,
It's turning, into, a dark day.

Trees curl over,
Like waves upon the shore.
Rain drips down,
On windows and doors.

A rumble of thunder,
Shakes the sky.
The rain beats down,
Like tears from my eye.

The leaves disappear in the darkness,
The rain spits down on the floor.
The wind wails through the clouds,
Getting a bit harder, some more.

The flashes of light continues,
The cracks of thunder goes on.
Fear inside children builds,
The bright blue skies have gone.

Katie Jayne Stone (12) Brecon High School

RAINBOW

I stand proudly,
Over the world,
Watching everything
That goes on.
When the birds fly past they sing
In my ear,
Singing their song.
Mostly warm am I,
I don't have a cold finger
Like snow.
Or wet like the rain,
I am just right.
My colours are beautiful,
When they reflect,
In the waters below,
Making the world look prettier.
Without me the world,
Wouldn't be colourful.

Michelle Lloyd (12) Brecon High School

IT

It glides through the water
Unseen by the human eye
Sightings of it have been seen
By visitors who to the Loch have been.

The Loch Ness monster is its name.
Who knows if it is wild or tame
We know it's big, we know it's alive
But how on earth does it survive?

Ben Sankala (12) Brecon High School

THE SUN

I'm the sun
Stuck in the sky,
I don't have much fun
In the sky so high.

I shine on all the people,
Down on the earth,
I am very, very, big,
But was a star at my birth.

I am very bored,
I'm the only boy in space,
All the stars are girls, and say,
I have a very ugly face.

I am very hot,
I am very bright,
I'm the only thing,
That'll give people light.

Timothy Morgan (12) Brecon High School

SWELL HEAD!

There's a boy called Swell Head
In my class and in the corridor
You cannot get passed.
His head will swell to the walls
You see, he squashes one then two and three.

When you look up in the sky
You see a balloon flying by,
And when it goes *pop!* It falls
Suddenly like a rocket going up,
But down and then it crashes
In Swell Head's home and Swell Head's
Head is beating with pain.

Huw Joseph (12) Brecon High School

IT

You can not see it with your eyes,
It's not invisible to your body.
It screams, it coughs, it sneezes
It yells and it cries through me.
It has travelled the world millions
of miles from one place to another.
It spreads, it has a never ending journey.
It has died many times but keeps coming
back again and again.
Soon it will die and never ever come back.
The future will kill it but only with
human help.

A Virus!

Amie Price (12) Brecon High School

MY CAR

Done a bit of wheelin' dealin',
Bought myself a car,
Stick the gear in now I'm steerin',
Gonna drive far in my car.

Been around the world in my car,
Driven hundreds and hundreds of miles,
Went out one night to a hotel bar,
Met a cool kinda guy called Giles.

He filled my car with gallons of beer,
Now my car won't go very fast,
Somehow my car is stuck in gear,
Now I've got rid of this guy at last.

Got myself home and fixed my car,
But it's still making a horrible sound,
I got myself some help and that's my pa,
Now it travels like lightning along the ground.

Now my car has just been sprayed,
In a colour resembling honey,
But I still have not yet paid,
Because I owe a lot of money.

Back came Giles to buy my car,
He thinks he's made a very good choice,
I'm not sure he'll go very far,
Meanwhile I'm drivin' my new Rolls Royce.

David Peter Molen (12) Brecon High School

IT

From its birth in the hills
It has gone through many glens,
Pushed watermills to grind the flour,
Along it goes giving life to the fields.
It passes through the town.
But it does not like the town.
Rubbish, muck and waste.
Then it is out in the open.
It is now old, nearly dying.
Then the sea a wild ferocious place.
Taking lives during storms.
The river is ending.
Its death place as large as the eye can see.

Thomas Penny (12) Brecon High School

IT

In winter he comes and strikes
his icy fingers all over the world.

He blows a frosty wind, wind which
leaves icicles hanging from the roof tops.

He casts a magical spell which
he will never tell, he is a terrifying
force of white which comes out at night.

Frost!

Hayley Hughes (12) Brecon High School

THE SUN

She lies in the sky all year round
She wakes early without a sound.
Then she stretches her sparkling arms of rays
Which give the whole world light for weeks and days.
Without her there life would not survive,
We rely on her to stay alive.
She gives us all our energy
And shines on things for us to see.
She hides in the clouds when it's due to rain
But soon it stops and she peeps out again.
She drinks the rain from puddles of water
Stopping the land from flooding below her.
She is praised by people from faraway lands
Because she makes miracles with her warm hands.
At the end of the day she descends to rest
She is the biggest star and the very best.

Elizabeth Thomas (13) Brecon High School

THE FIELD MOUSE

I see its silhouetted body,
Against the calm red sky,
Moving with the straw,
With a glimmer in its eye.

I can't hear it, just the straw and the wind,
As he crawls up and up so determined,
To get to the top, and get to the wheat,
For him it's something nice to eat.

So he nibbles a little,
And takes some back down,
For a mini feast,
Under the ground.

In his burrow he is safe,
Unlike outside,
Where danger lurks,
But he's warm inside.

The sun is now up,
The red sky has gone,
Now life has begun,
But for the field mouse,
Who was out all night,
He goes to sleep,
And curls up tight.

Mike Dunn (13) Brecon High School

SIMPLY ME

I am a secret person,
I like the colour black, it's mysterious,
The night is silent for looking at the stars,
When it is night and lightning, that's what I like.
I would be a great big arm chair
People can sit in me all day.
Salad I like, it's nice and fresh,
If there was a fire I would grab an old ring and family.
Shorts and T-shirts big and baggy I am.
My favourite things are cats and dogs.
I hate it when I come home,
The food is gone when my brother is there.
I wish I could be famous for designing hats.

Amber Pimm-Jones (11) John Beddoes School

SIMPLY ME

I'm an oak desk with many drawers
and secret compartments,
I like mysterious things.
What irritates me is my brother when he
eats crunchy food.
I am sunny and cloudy,
I get bored easily.

I'm a mid morning person,
I wake fully at about ten o'clock,
In a fire at home I would grab
either my walkman or my computer,
I'm a jeans and T-shirt person,
No fuss and simple,
I'm a green person because I like animals.

Jacob Greenwood (11) John Beddoes School

THE LESSON

Today I have a cookery class,
I will need some dishes of china and glass.

What shall I do?
What shall I wear?
The apron with Snoopy on,
Or Pudsy Bear?

As I climb the classroom stairs,
I smell the aroma of chocolate eclairs.

I open the door and walk on in,
Someone is spilling flour from a tin.

As it cascades,
It covers the floor,
The teacher exclaims, 'I can't stand any more!'

Then once again there is peace in the kitchen,
And teacher's lip has finally stopped twitching.

Next I shall need some flour and marg,
Then two baking tins, one small, one large.

I make a cake and mix it well,
And open the oven door to smell,
Other pupils' baking almost done,
Baking a cake has been quite fun!

Amy Parfitt (12) John Beddoes School

NO PAIN NO GAIN

No pain, no gain, that's what I was told,
As I entered the gym, feeling very bold,
New socks and shorts, the very latest vest,
I had to make sure, I was looking my best.

I'd come to pump some iron, shift a little fat,
That's the theory, if only I could lift it
Off the mat.
I was in the correct position, to do the perfect lift,
The only thing stopping me, was the weight that
Wouldn't shift.

Well I huff and puff, puff and pant,
If you can you can, but if you can't you can't,
The only thing I've pulled, is a muscle,
And boy it aches,
The only things I'll be lifting now,
Are Cadbury's chocolate cakes.

Claire Chillery (12) John Beddoes School

SIMPLY ME

I'm a light blue like the Lone Ranger
A night person like a bat - creepy, eerie, sinister
The army jeans and T-shirt type I crave adventure,
I'm the DIY table quick and simple.
I'm that day which you don't know what's going to happen,
The cocktail a mixture of feelings,
A fish and chips greasy but still crisp,
A tree climber, a monkey that grips,
The cop that used his life to save someone else.

Jon Turner (11) John Beddoes School

SIMPLY ME

I am the colour green, it is calm and cheerful.
I am seven o'clock in the morning,
Ready to start the day.
A colourful salad, bright and refreshing,
I will be remembered
The greatest parachutist ever!
My favourite things are my coins,
Foreign ones,
Viking ones,
Types of all different kinds.
I am an old Roman clock,
Ancient, yet working.
What irritates me is my brother,
He calls me names.
If there was a fire I would grab,
My old lighter given to me by my Dad.

Andrew Middleton (11) John Beddoes School

SIMPLY ME

A green colour for me,
All for helping the environment,
A jeans person,
With a baggy T-shirt,
I'm simple,
No fuss,
Chips are simple,
Like me,
Just simple,
Easy going,
Coke is for me,
I'm easy,
No fuss
I'm a night person,
Like an owl
I'm like a soft chair,
I would save my family,
Not toys,
People grinding their teeth,
I hate it,
I love my family,
My pets too,
Most of all my family,
I'm sun and rain,
On and off,
Cheerful then moody,
I would like to be remembered,
For saving the rain forests,
And the environment.

Rebecca Hall (11) John Beddoes School

SIMPLY ME

I am jet black like Christmas Eve's night.
I am a sunny day, most of the time.
I love one thing the most and that's my family.
I am a loose T-shirt or denim jeans
Simple, quick, ordinary.
I am a 7 o'clock happy in the morning.
I am a roast dinner or a fresh colourful salad.
A hot cup of chocolate, that's me.
Hot, frothy, just right on a cold winter's eve.

Isabel Morris (11) John Beddoes School

SIMPLY ME!

I'm really a happy kind of person,
I come alive at five,
I'm a black mysterious kind of girl.

If there was a fire,
All I would grab is my family,
I want to be remembered by
helping people as well as animals,
I'm a baggy clothes kind of person,
Always on the run,
I'm always eating chocolate cake
in front of the TV.

I'm dreaming I'm a painting
on an important wall,
polished every day by my owner.

Lee O'Rourke (11) John Beddoes School

ME

I love my horse and ring
Given to me exactly one year ago,
I'm a mid-day person - ready for lunch
I'm a long antique table, polished to shine.
I'm a choc full - bar of milk choc
plenty of calories!
I'm an orange juice drinker when I
start I just can't stop.
I'm a jean kind of person
that runs like the wind
I'd like to be remembered as a
John Whittaker and Milton a millionaire
light blue pale and cool, like the sea.

Bethan Davies (11) John Beddoes School

SIMPLY ME

I love guinea pigs they're soft, warm and cuddly,
I don't like my sister she's annoying me.
If a fire started, I would rush to their cage to get them out.
If I was a piece of furniture I would be a pillow, soft and bright
with colours.
The time of day I like the best is home time, so that I can relax.
My favourite type of food is corn on the cob.
Why? You ask.
I like it with a bit of butter.
If I was a piece of clothing I'd be a track suit, nice and baggy.
If I was a type of weather I would be sunny and warm.
The colour I would be is red to represent the sunset at nightfall.
I would like to be remembered as a kind person, not a horrible one.

Demelsa Hopkins (12) John Beddoes School

THE JOYS OF THE SEA

The sound of the sea,
Appeals to me,
Any day of my life.

The fluffy white sky,
That meets your eye,
It matches the calm blue sea.

The horrific great waves,
That smash against the caves,
On a thundering stormy night;
Climb up the rocks and cling on tight,
The tremendous great waves,
Can cause such a fright.

One minute it's the sun,
But now it's the lightning,
Striking the cliffs,
It's really quite frightening.

Bethan Lusher (12) John Beddoes School

THE POEM ABOUT ME

Help me there is a fire in
my house I'll grab a
ten pence and go to a phone box
and dial 999.

I come from out of a motorbike shop
with this denim jacket on and
some grey jeans on.

I am a four o'clock person that's
when I come out from
school happy as anything can be

I am a yellow person I
try to be happy but
I am sometimes black
and at home my sister gets on my
nerves, or I get growled or get
told off.

I am a coke person that's
why coke fizzes up
in your mouth.

Colin Bufton (12) John Beddoes School

SIMPLY ME

I love my bike, my rabbits
and my computers,
I'd grab any thing I could in
an emergency,
If I could be a fruit
I would be a passion fruit
because people like them,
If it was possible I would
be a denim jacket,
Most people like me are a
4.00 person it's hometime!
I'm a normal weather person
not too hot not too cold just right,
I'd like to be yellow because yellow
is bright I'm not,
I wish I could be the
Mona Lisa because it's special,
When I die I want to be remembered
as a nice person that
every one liked.

Joshua Traylor (11) John Beddoes School

SIMPLY ME

A mid-day person,
Dead when I wake up,
I quickly transform,
To a happy sunny day,
Ready to run like the wind,
An antique table polished to shine.
Liked to be remembered as a dancer
A model a Manchester United fan.
I picture myself as a cup of coffee,
Nice and hot,
With evaporating steam,
Going going gone.

Maddy Wozencraft (11) John Beddoes School

SIMPLY ME

I shine like the sun
My favourite colour is orange
I am happy at 4.00pm
When school ends
I wear jeans a lot
They're casual
Easy to wear
I like chips and beans
They're simple
I would like to be remembered
As a cheerful person
I'm easy no fuss
I like hot chocolate
It's creamy on the top
My favourite animal is a pussy cat.

Diane Jones (11) John Beddoes School

SIMPLY ME

I am a soft bouncy sofa.
With scarlet velvet covering.
You might want to sit down.
But be warned, scarlet has its dangers
My springs are a bit rusty.
I'm not perfect.

I am a warm summer evening person.
I hope I'm kind but I can get angry.
My clothes are fashionable but casual.
I am a hot steamy Sunday lunch,
I like to take my time.
Sunday lunch takes a long time to cook.
The one thing in the world that irritates me
Is fidgeting I hate it!

Tilly Langton (11) John Beddoes School

SIMPLY ME

I'm a baking hot sun
glazing down on people
Giving them a sun burn.
I give people a smile.
Their hair has gone to
a different colour from me.

I'm a denim person
Ready for anything. I'm
always on time for a
party, all because
my denim jacket, I'm
always ready

I'm greasy chips and
sausage, ready to get
eaten to get people's
clothes all greasy,
never let them avoid me.

Philip Morrell (11) John Beddoes School

INFORMATION

We hope you have enjoyed reading this book - and that you will continue to enjoy it in the coming years.

If you like reading and writing poetry drop us a line, or give us a call, and we'll send you a free information pack.

Poetry Now (Young Writers) Information
1-2 Wainman Road
Woodston
Peterborough
PE2 7BU